Circle of Solace

a coloring book

72 coloring pages

by ColorAnyTime

www.coloranytime.com

Introduction

Nothing gives more pleasure and relaxation than coloring.

It's all about having some time to yourself and creating something unique. You decide the colors, you decide which page to do today and there is no right or wrong way to do it.

You can even cut the page out and frame it as it is!

Most importantly, have fun!

The images can be colored by the whole family.

This publication is part of a series of products and publications. For more information, please visit: http://www.coloranytime.com/.

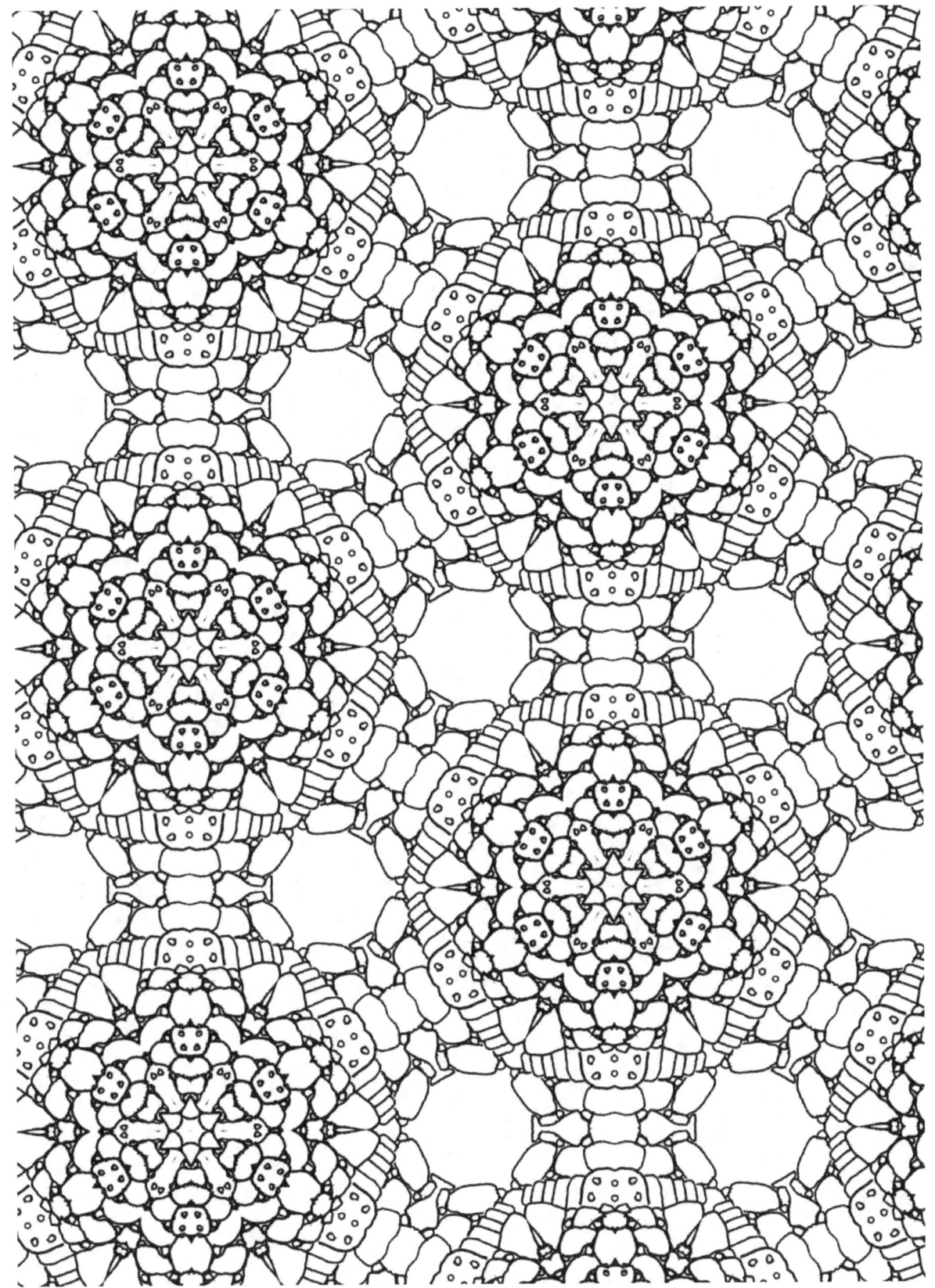

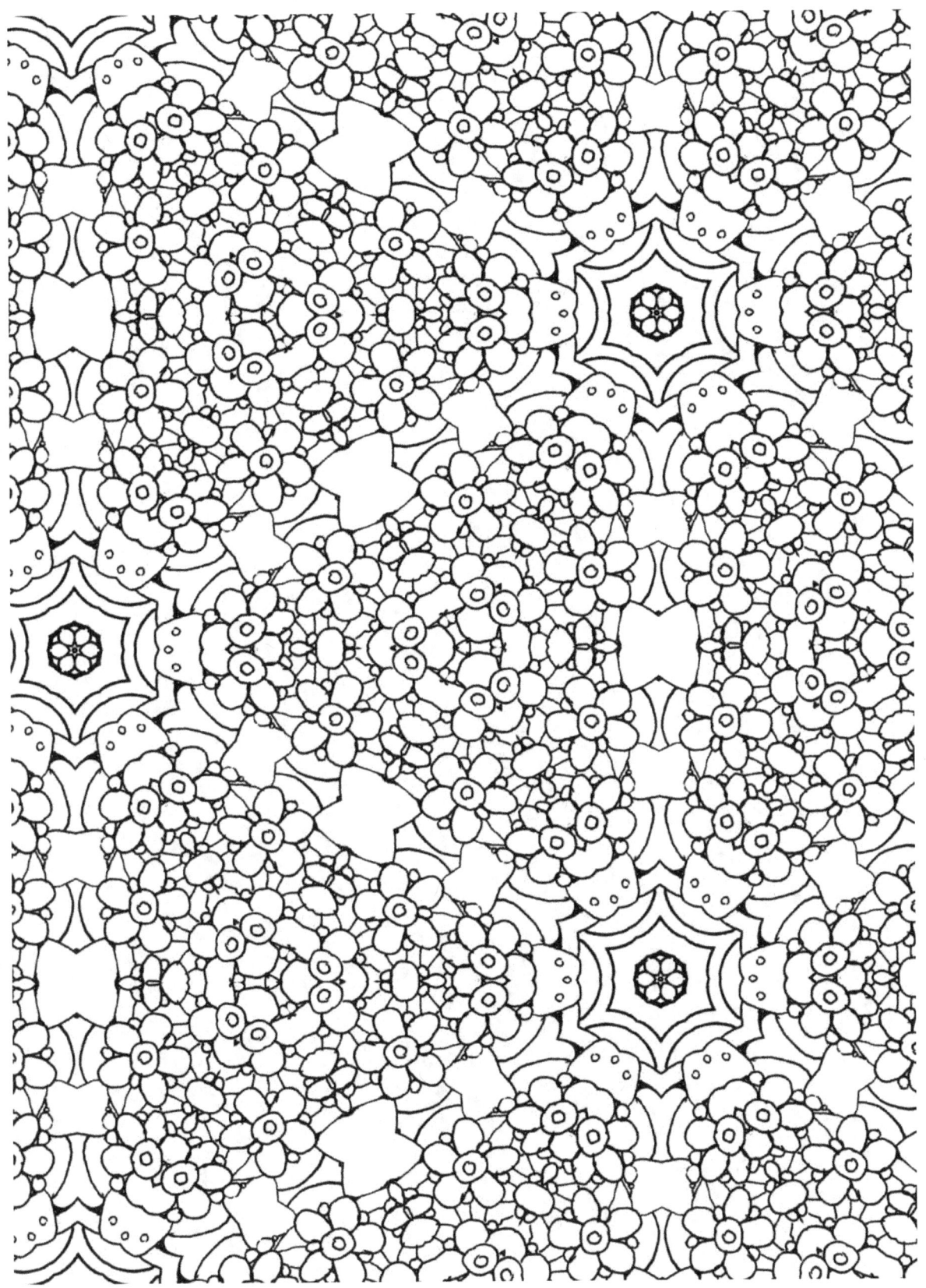

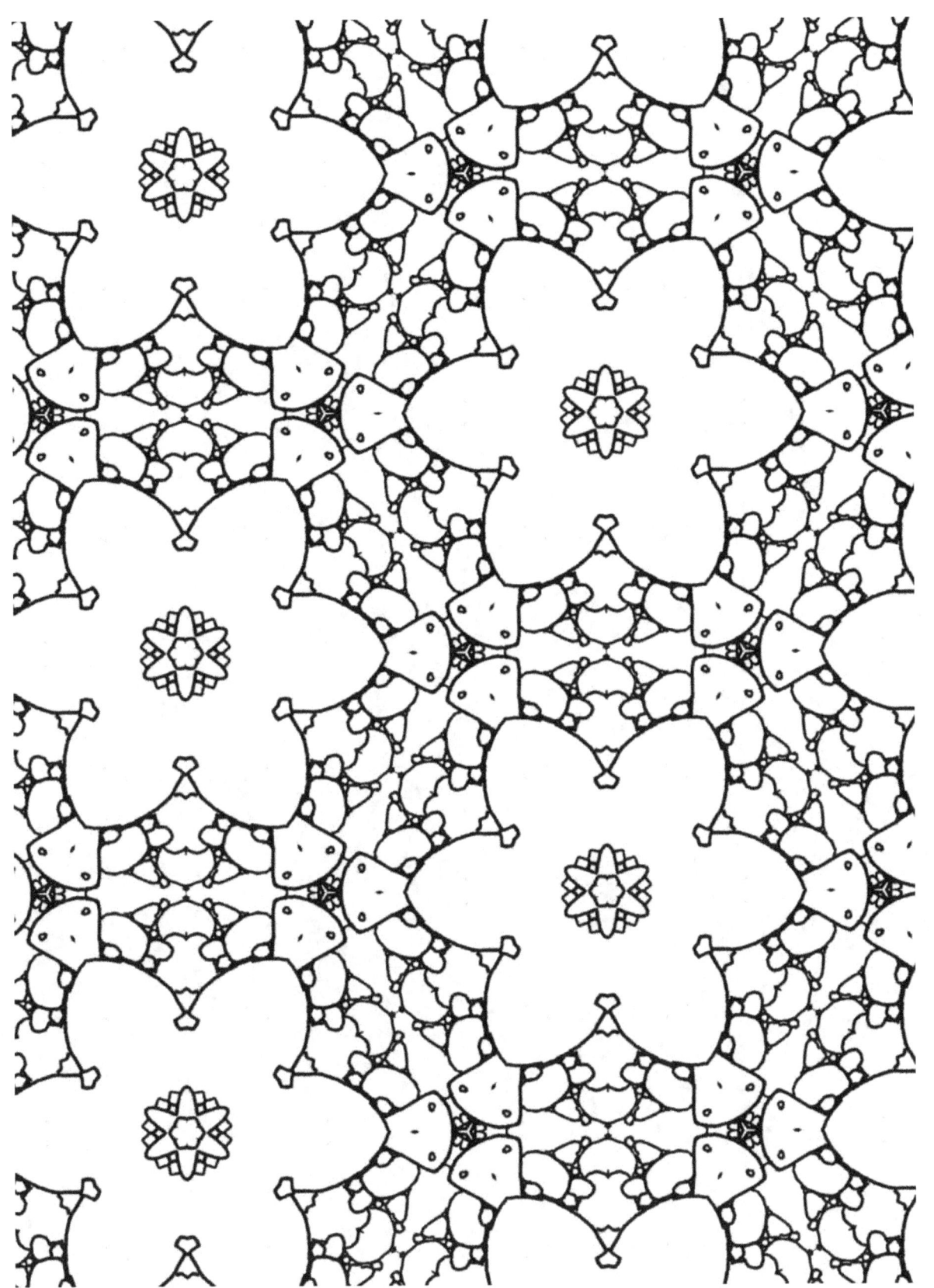

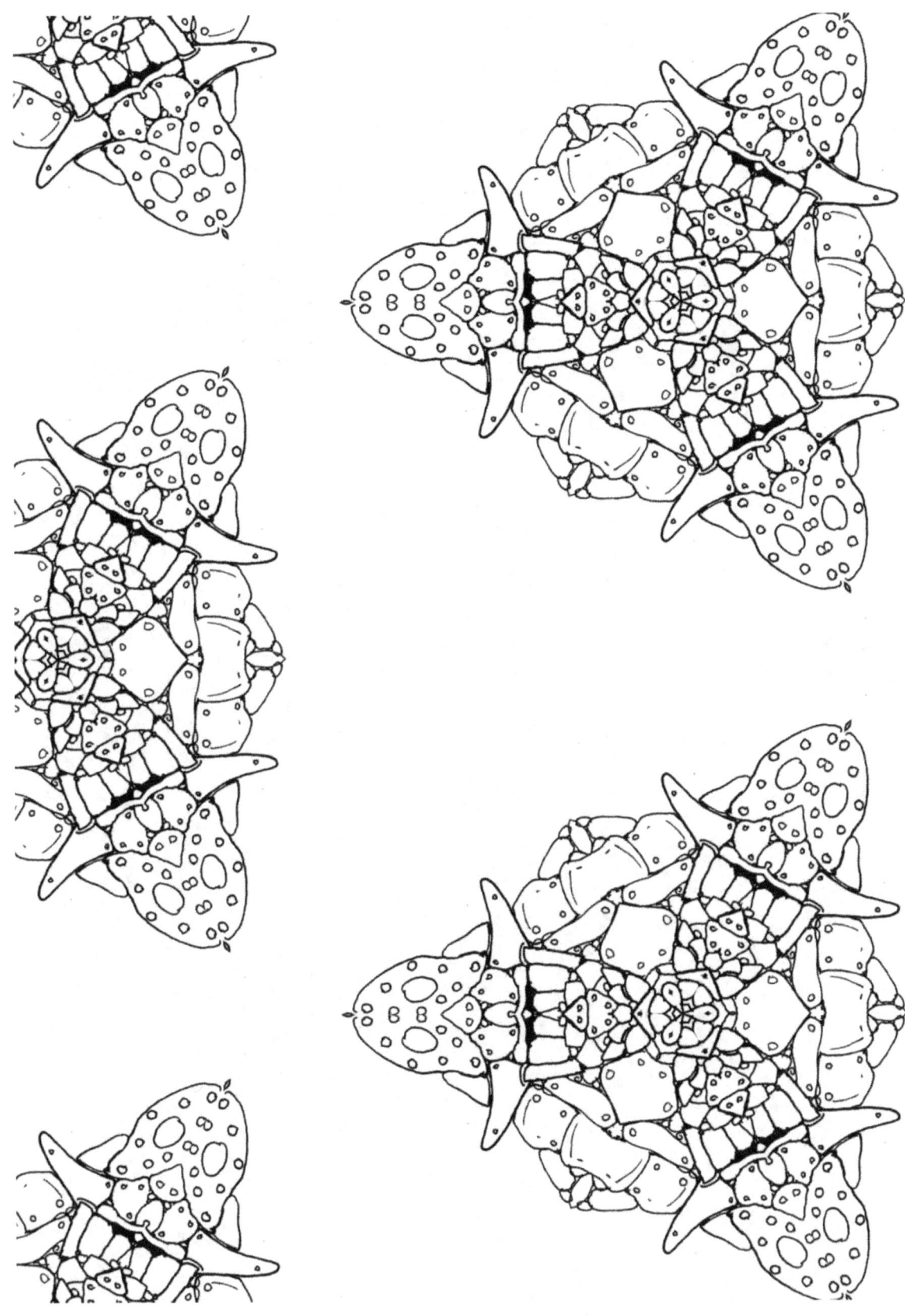

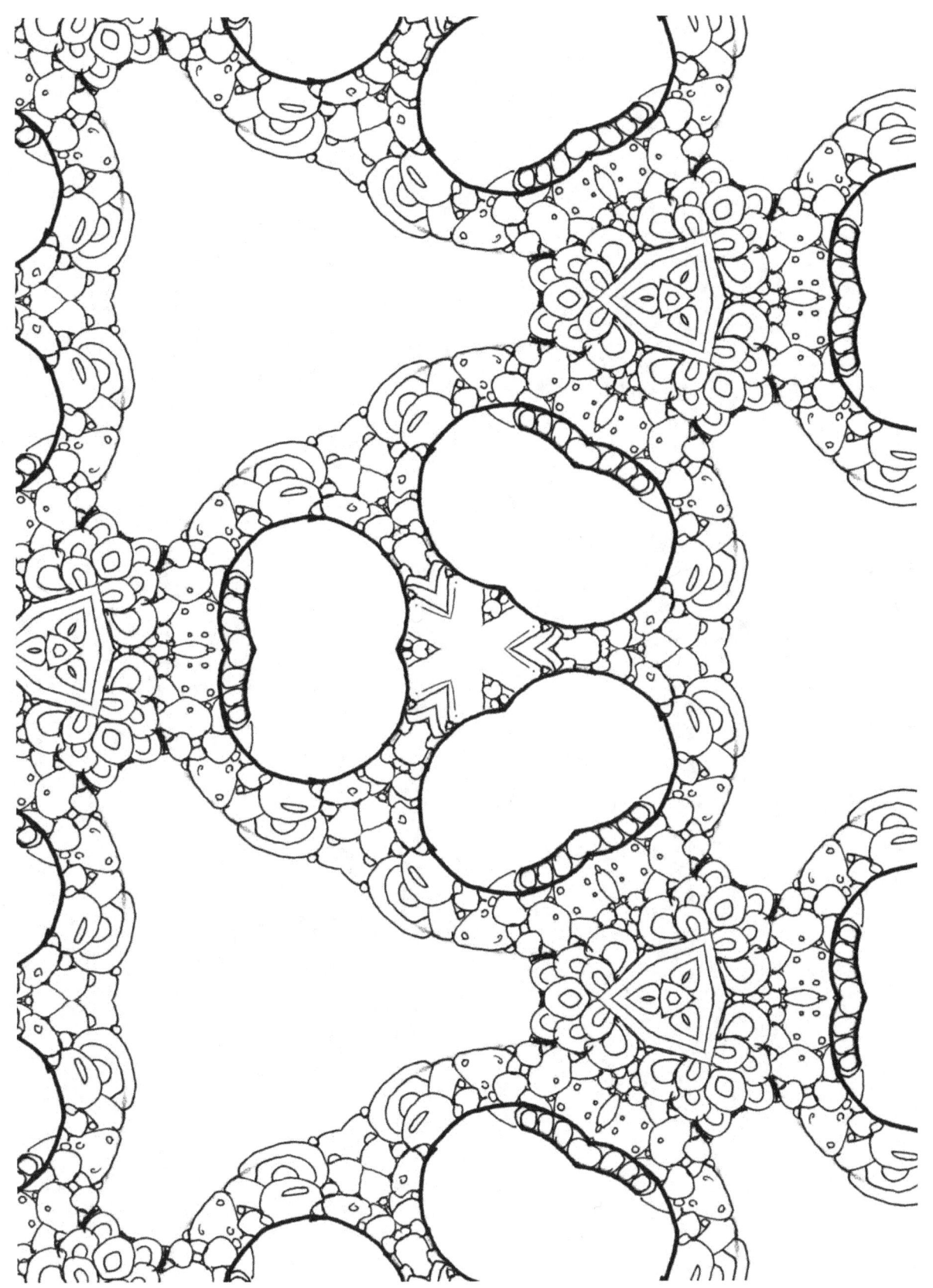

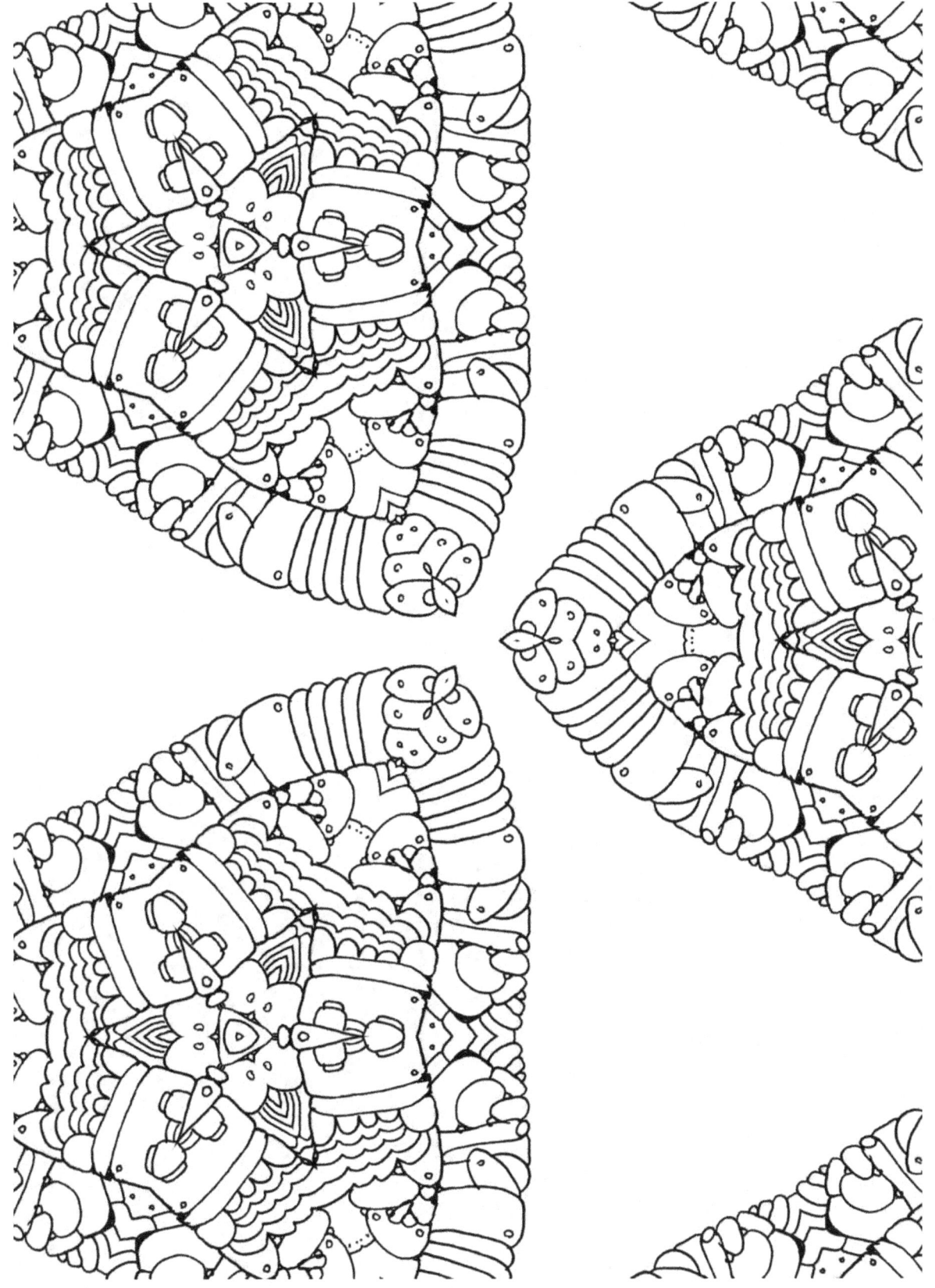

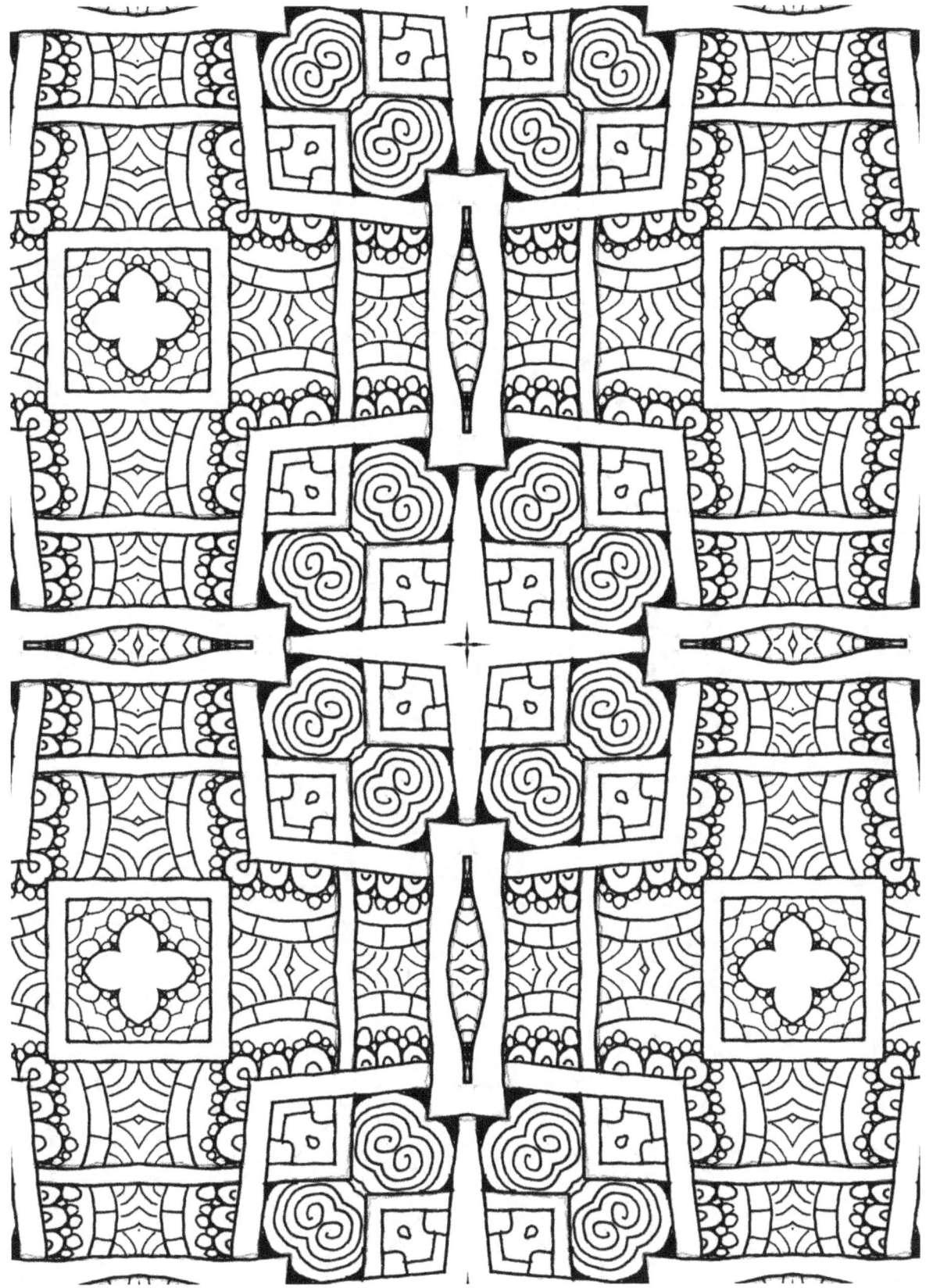

I truly hope you have enjoyed this book!

For more info visit our website:

www.coloranytime.com